Alice in the News

Charles Way

NT   Barrington Stoke

Introduction

The play you are about to read is brought to you through a sparkling new writing programme called Assembly. It is one of a series of five new works by world-class writers written specially for children to perform. The plays were originally commissioned by the National Theatre in collaboration with Camden Action Zone. We wanted to create brilliant scripts that a whole class could perform as part of a special, primary school, extended assembly or as a school production, which could also provide a rich and thought provoking focus for cross-curricular work. So we approached some of our favourite writers and asked them to write their next play much as they would any other; but, for a cast as big as they could imagine and with younger characters in mind. We said we wanted the scripts to be no less sophisticated than the adult work with which they are more commonly associated and full of invention and theatrical challenge. Alice in the News is also suitable for use in Year 7 and Year 8.

It became very evident early on that there is a real hunger for well-crafted scripts for the very young to explore. This is why Assembly has now become a nation-wide programme currently spearheaded by the National in partnership with Theatre Royal Plymouth, a consortium of major theatres, the publisher Barrington Stoke, the DfES and schools and Creative Partnerships throughout the UK.

You'll see that the publisher has invented a brand new way of making this script easily accessible to even the most reluctant reader. We'd like the play to be staged as well as read and so it is accompanied by helpful tips based on a series of workshops led by Rebecca Gould and her team at Theatre Royal Plymouth. Assembly is part of the National Theatre's Connections programme. Connections develop scripts for the secondary school age range. A further series of Assembly is now in development. If you'd like to see them or be part of the Assembly programme visit the Connection's web-site on www.shellconnections.org.uk

Suzy Graham-Adriani
National Theatre
January 2004

Name: Charles Way

Play: Alice in the News

When did you first start to write plays?

I started when I was 14 writing plays that the school put on. I've been a professional playwright since I was 23. I've never really done any other kind of work.

How many plays have you written?

I've written over 40 plays and all but two of them have been produced. I do some TV and radio stuff but theatre is what I love.

Do you write for all ages?

Yes. I try to write plays that don't exclude anyone. If they are for young people they can still have depth and adults can get something from them.

Who is your favourite audience?

My favourite audience would be one with a mixture of age groups.

Do you always go and watch your plays?

I always go to see my plays. I believe in the rehearsal process and going through it with the actors. Generally, my experience has been positive. This business is about trusting others and working together.

Do you wish you could choose the actors for your plays?
I sometimes get involved in auditions but it is not enjoyable. It can be painful and cruel and anyway, casting is a very special skill.

Who is your favourite character in this play?
Alice, of course. But there are others. There's a scientist who comes off the obituary page but he can't read his own obituary and therefore he doesn't know who he is. Alice has to find out by asking him questions.

Are there any scenes in this play you would have liked acted in a particular way?
I would like the end to be as dramatic and as tense as possible. Alice is sentenced to be questioned to death by two question marks and she is asked stupid questions like, 'What is the end of the Circle Line?' In the end she just rips up the newspaper and frees herself from the mad universe she's in.

What is your favourite play?
The Winter's Tale by William Shakespeare. It is not a perfect play but it is full of wonderful juxtapositions.

Do you write books as well?
No. I just write plays.

Did you read a lot at school?
When we were at school we had a rest period every day and I used to read. When I was 12 I started *Lorna Doone* by R.D. Blackmore. It was the first book I had read that reflected my experience as a boy from Devon. I loved it and I have been hooked on reading ever since.

Interview by Jim Mulligan

Characters

Alice

Dad

 Woman

 Someone

The Consonants:

 N

 W

 S

 F

 D

The Vowels:

 A

 I

 O

 U

 E

Exclamation Marks:

 EX 1

 EX 2

 Model

Children:

 Child 1

 Child 2

 Ballerina

 Cricketer

 Scientist

Question Marks:

 QM 1

 QM 2

 QM 3

Music. Alice is walking to school. She walks on the spot, going nowhere fast. As she speaks, she sees the very thing she is describing.

Alice

My name is Alice.

I'm walking to school

and I'm thinking about Dad.

Because this morning I said, 'Hello Dad',

and he said nothing, nothing at all.

He just kept on reading his newspaper.

And then I saw that his face had gone all white

and I said, ? 'What's the matter? What's happened?'

And he said –

Dad

Nothing – nothing at all.

Alice

? Nothing?

Dad

Nothing important.

Her father, behind his newspaper, now becomes one of the people who Alice describes at the bus stop.

Alice	So now I'm walking to school
	and see a woman at the bus stop.
	Every day she says,
Woman	"Hello Alice"
Alice	But today, she too has a white face.
	She too is reading a newspaper and frowning.
	She's so busy frowning she doesn't even see me.
	Now the bus comes and it's very odd
	because everyone is so quiet.
	They're all reading their newspapers
	and looking serious and shocked
	as if something terrible has happened.
	And now the bus stops
	and everyone gets off
	and no one says anything,
	which is strange.
	Someone always says something like –

 **Someone** "I'll see you later"

Alice Or –

 **Someone** "Lovely weather"

Alice Even when it's not.

But today is different, and a bit scary

So I tell myself to be brave and say –

"Excuse me".

"? Has something happened?"

"? Why is everyone frowning?"

The people with newspapers hear her and turn away.

Alice ! Excuse me!

Still no one speaks. They become a wall of silence –
a wall of newspapers. She tries to get in to see what
they are reading but they will not let her.

Alice ! Excuse me!

Alice stands there, puzzled and rather angry.
Suddenly a sharp cold wind blows across the street.
Everyone except Alice is blown away down the street.
Alice stands quite still in the face of the howling gale.
Just Alice and many sheets of newspaper are left.
She goes up to one sheet of newspaper rather
nervously. She slowly picks it up. It has a hole in it.
She climbs into the hole. And that's when it happens.
With a sudden cry and a strange sucking noise Alice
falls in a spin into the newspaper. She spins and spins
like a top. When she finally stops, she gazes about in
wonder. There is a moment's silence then she hears
the sound of feet. Moving very gracefully, several
letters enter.

[This may be as simple as an actor with a large letter on his or her chest, capitals on the back – lower case letters on the front. If there are a lot of actors to fit in the whole alphabet could enter doing a simple step dance.]

The letters form the words, 'The Daily News'.
Alice creeps up to them from behind, but suddenly the
letter 'a' swaps places with the letter 'e', making 'The
Diely Naws', which than becomes 'The Daly Niwees'.
The Consonants start to look nervous.

N   ? What are you doing?

W   Get back into line.

N   All of you.

S   You'll get us into trouble.

W   ! Stop it! Stop it!

A   For Freedom.

*At this battle cry, a fight breaks out between the
Vowels and the Consonants, as the Consonants try
to stop the Vowels from leaving the words.
Alice is caught in the middle of this and hides under
the sheets of newspaper. A drum beat is then heard,
all freeze for a moment.*

A   ! Run – Run!

*A line of four Exclamation Marks enter to the sound of
a drum beat. The Vowels escape.*

The leader of the Exclamation Marks – EX 1, shouts some orders which no one can understand in a Sergeant Major style. EX 1 is wearing a hat which looks like a policeman's helmet.

 **EX 1**   Bring 'em in to line. One two, one two, one two.

The Exclamation Marks have little exclamation mark style batons, they surround the Consonants, who shrink back in fright.

 **EX 1**   So it's happened. I always feared it would.

F   It wasn't our fault.

All   It was the Vowels. The Vowels.

 **EX 1**   ? And where are the Vowels? Hey?

D   We tried to stop them.

N   But they just keep running away.

S   And they had someone with them –

 **EX1**   ? What do you mean – a picture of someone?

S   It could have been – but she was more – just like – someone.

EX1   This is a newspaper, we have words and we have pictures – and sometimes when they're not running away we have letters. We don't have someones. Take 'em away.

EX 2   By the left – March!

Exclamation Mark 1 looks around and just misses seeing Alice.

EX1   ? Someone hey? How very odd. *[Exit]*

Alice slowly looks up. She sees the Vowels coming back and hides under the paper again. The Vowels enter, their faces now smeared with camouflage paint, and carrying guns – they come on stage nervously.

A   ? I?

I   Yes A.

A   ? Where are we?

I   Looks like fashion.

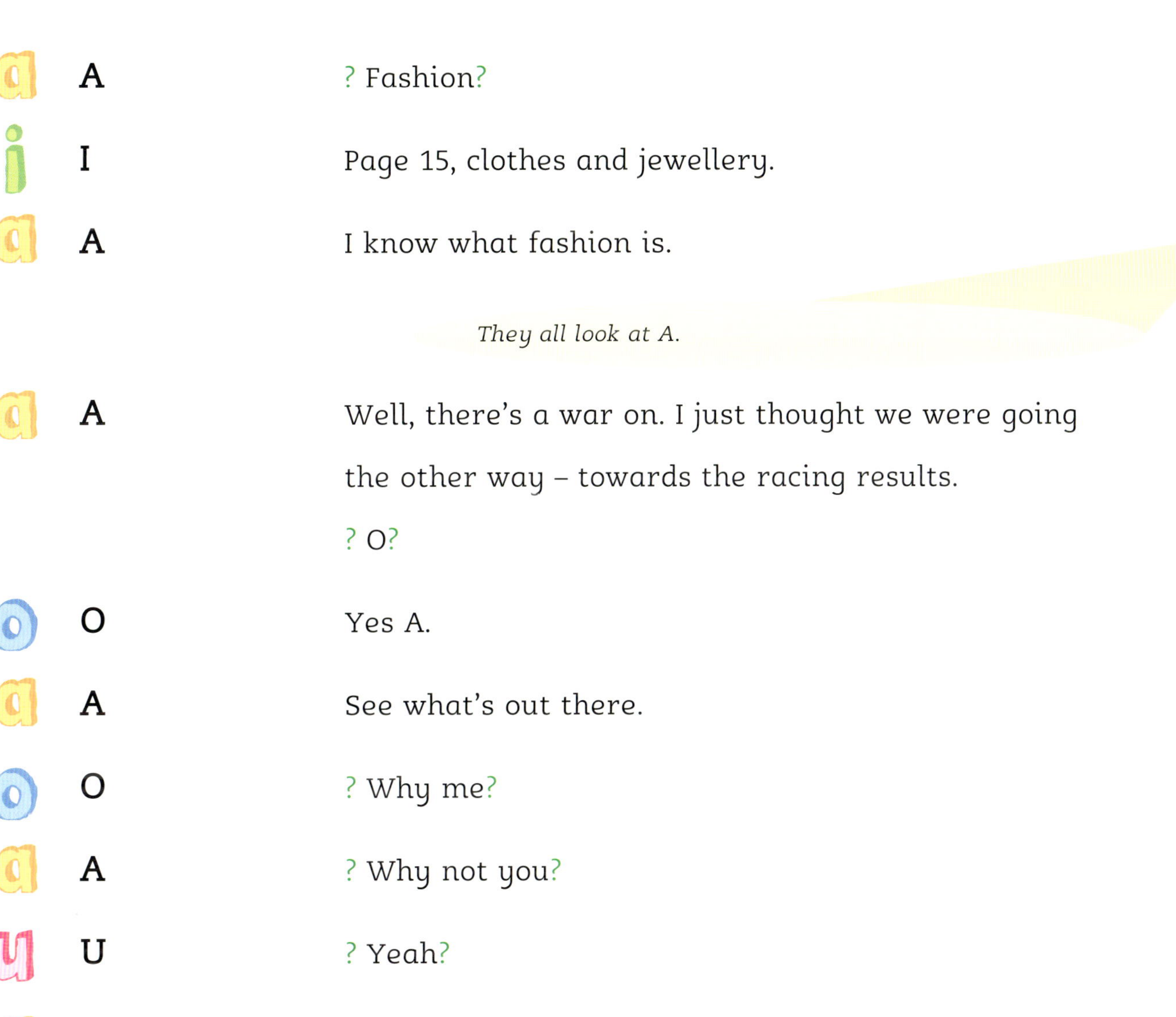

	A	? Fashion?
	I	Page 15, clothes and jewellery.
	A	I know what fashion is.

They all look at A.

	A	Well, there's a war on. I just thought we were going the other way – towards the racing results. ? O?
	O	Yes A.
	A	See what's out there.
	O	? Why me?
	A	? Why not you?
	U	? Yeah?
	A	No, not you U. O.
	U	Oh.

O   ? Yeah?

A   No – for pity's sake, just go.

O   Right.

O runs out – looks around – comes back.

A   ? Anything?

O   Nothing. *[Sadly]* Just a pile of yesterday's.*

*yesterday's = Past newspapers and past memories

A   All right. The last page they'll look is the page we just left – so relax. Take five everyone.

They all stand – and stretch. They gather round the newspapers under which Alice is hiding.

A   ? Got any grub?

E   ? What – don't you know there's a war on?

They all laugh in a friendly way. E pulls out a brown paper bag. He hands round what looks like sweets.

I   ? A?

A   Yeah. ? What?

I   There's somebody's foot.

> *Alice suddenly sits up and the Vowels scream.*
> *Alice screams. They scream again and point their*
> *guns at her. One doesn't have a gun but a cricket bat.*
> *She raises her hands.*

Alice   ! Don't shoot! Don't shoot!

E   It's a girl.

A   Shut up.

E   But it's a girl.

A   ? And what are you, a bloomin' midwife? I can see it's a girl.

O   ? What's she doing here?

A   ? Who are you? Why are you here? What do you want?

Alice   Well I – I don't know why I'm here – or what I want …

and anyway I might ask the same of you.

| Alice | ? Who are you? Why are you here? |

? And why are you pointing those guns at me? 

They put down the guns, looking rather ashamed.

A — Well – we only just got them.

I — They were on the international page.

O — Just lying there.

Alice — Well you shouldn't point them at anyone.

After all you're just letters.

I — ? Just letters? Just Letters? Of course we're just letters.

E — Just like you're a girl.

O — In the wrong place – at the wrong time.

A — All right – all right. Calm it down. We're all a bit nervous.

I — Been on the run.

Alice — ? What are you running from?

A   ? Don't you know anything?

O   We're the resistance.

I   The only hope left. ? What's your name?

Alice   Alice.

A   Nice name.

E   Three good vowels.

A   Yeah – Alice is a nice word to be in.

           ? But not all words are nice – are they? It's the words you see.

U   The terrible words.

A   Words you wouldn't want to be in.

E   ? How would you feel everyday to be in words like –

           like ... I can't even say them ?

Alice   I'm sorry, but I never knew that letters had feelings,

           or thoughts – or anything.

A   Well, that just goes to show how little you know.

Alice Well, I … it's all very new. And a bit … *[She breaks down in tears]*

A ! Oh dear! We've made her cry.

E No - you made her cry.

A Well, it's no good crying girl - not in times like these.

U Here – ? perhaps you'd like a bite to eat?

Alice *[Feeling a bit better]* Thank you – ? what are they?

U Full stops – ? like em?

Alice I'm not sure. I mean – I've never eaten a full stop before, so I don't know what it's meant to taste like.

A ? Never been in the news before have you?

Alice No, and though it's interesting, and nice to meet you of course – really – I'd just like to go home.

A ? Home? This is no time to think about home. We are in the middle of a great rebellion.

I We can't let the words rule us anymore.

| O | ! Freedom for all letters! |

| All | ! Freedom! |

| Alice | But – forgive me for saying – ? isn't that the whole point of being letters – to be in words? |

Silence. They stare at her.

| I | Someone's coming. |

| A | You tell them Alice that we'll fight in every column – every page, every story – for our … our … |

| I | Independence. |

| Alice | ? Tell who? |

| U | You really do not know a thing. |

| Alice | I assure you I know quite a few things – actually. |

| U | ? Oh yeah? But you don't how you got here or how to get out – ? – do you – actually? |

I Come on. Come on.

Exit Vowels. Enter a Fashion Model, in a ridiculous outfit. She sees Alice.

Model You there. Yes, you.

She hobbles over in high heeled shoes and sunglasses, which she takes off to look at Alice.

? And what kind of fashion do you call that?

Alice I don't.

Model Neither do I dear. Oh, this really won't do – it won't do at all. I have no idea what's going on. ? Do you?

Alice No.

Model There was some dreadful shouting, and now I don't know who I am anymore.

Alice It's something to do with the Vowels.

Model ? Vowels?

| Alice | I can't really explain it, but it seems very important. |

| Model | ? Do you know your name? |

| Alice | Yes. |

| Model | ? Do you know my name? |

| Alice | No. |

| Model | ! Then, what good are you! |

| Alice | Surely, you know your own name. |

| Model | My name was under my picture – suddenly the name vanished. All I was left with was Cld. ? What kind of name is that? |

| Alice | ? You're a picture? |

| Model | Of course I'm a picture. ? Aren't you? |

| Alice | No. |

| Model | Well, I am. I'm a picture of someone famous and beautiful, called Cld – and I'm very, very upset. |

Alice   I'm sure there are more important things in the world
to be upset about.

Model   ? How dare you?

She takes a swing at Alice with her handbag.

Alice   ! Ow!

Model   Serves you right.

*She stomps off. Drum beat – Alice pretends to be a
photograph of a fashion Model. She stands as still as
she can. Enter EX 1 and 2.*

EX 1   Slippery, sly, little Vowels.
So – they came back into fashion.

EX 1 thinks this very funny.

It's not funny – look.   *[He picks up the brown paper bag}*

EX 2   Poor little full stops, ? what did they ever do to anybody?
When I catch those Vowels I'm going to …   *[He punches the air]*

 **EX 2**   and then I'm going to … *[He kicks an imaginary vowel]*

? How could they?

 **EX 1**   I don't know son. All my life I have tried to keep things in order – in shape. Shape and order that's what it's all about. But now this … it's the beginning of the end.

Enter the Model.

 **Model**   You there. Yes you.

 **EX 1**   Oh dear. Now then – keep polite – shape and order.

? Yes Madam?

 **Model**   ? What's going on? Nothing makes any sense.

I don't know who I am.

 **EX 1**   Please don't panic Mam.

 **Model**   But I am panicking. ? Can't you see?

 **EX 1**   The safest thing is to stay put.

Model   ? What do you mean? Am I not not safe? – Why am I not safe?

 **EX 1** And your identity will be returned to you as soon as possible. In the meantime don't go wandering from page to page. We don't want all the pictures running round the paper – cause a right panic.

 **Model** I know – it's her fault.

They look at Alice.

Model She's not a picture. She's an intruder. She's she's …

EX 1 She's the someone.

Alice screams, and starts running on the spot – getting nowhere fast.

EX 1 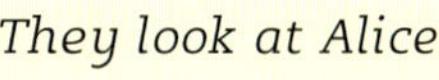 ! Well don't just stand there – catch her!

The Exclamation Marks and the Model are running behind her – they almost catch her but one falls so they drop back. Alice keeps running. A football team in a red strip join her. They keep running. Then they turn and run with their backs to the audience and their names on their shirts have the vowels missing, e.g. Mchl wn etc. They exit.

Alice   ? Hello?

  **Children**   ? Who are you?

Alice   Alice.

  **Children**   ? What page are you from?

Alice   I'm not – I'm just … ? what page are you from?

Child 1   We don't know.

Child 2   But we don't want to go back there.

Child 1   Please don't make us go back there.

Child 2   There were bombs falling.

Child 1   And people lying down.

Child 2   And nothing to eat.

25

  **Children**   Please don't make us go back there.

 **Child 1**   We'll go with you. ? Can we?

The chasing pack, which is made up of the Exclamation Marks, the Model and some footballers, appears in the distance.

Alice   No I … I have to … to run.

She keeps running on the spot. Once again, she loses the chasing pack. Now a Ballerina dances across the stage and joins her for a moment.

 **Ballerina**   Hello.

Alice   Hello.

 **Ballerina**   ? Have you read the reviews?

Alice   No.

   **Ballerina**   Nor me – I was about to when they vanished.

Alice   It's something to do with the Vowels.

 **Ballerina**

I can only think that I was brilliant.

If only I knew what ballet it was.

Alice

I'm sure it was very good.

 **Ballerina**

I don't think you should have opinions about a ballet

you haven't even seen.

She dances off. Alice keeps running.
A line of people in suits and hard hats join her as she
runs and jumps from page to page. A cricket player
without a bat runs with her for a few moments.

 **Cricketer**

? Have you seen my cricket bat?

Alice

No.

Exit Cricketer.

Alice

I mean yes.

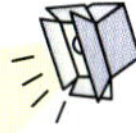

She stops running. She is alone. She has left the
chasing pack behind. Now a scientist in a white coat
with a walking stick wanders on, looking puzzled.

Alice ? Hello?

Scientist Hello there. All very odd.

Alice Yes.

Scientist Very confusing.

Alice Very.

Scientist Still – least it's quiet now.

Alice Yes.

Scientist ? Did you hear gunshots earlier?

Alice ? Gunshots?

Scientist ? I was wondering if there was some sort of conflict going on?

Alice Yes. Something terrible has happened.

I knew it first thing this morning – before I …

Scientist How scary.

Alice It's to do with the Vowels.

| Scientist | ? The Vowels? |

| Alice | They've got guns and one's got a cricket bat. |

| Scientist | That doesn't seem strictly necessary. |

| Alice | And there are pictures running all over the paper, trying to find out who they are. |

| Scientist | I find myself in the same position. When I arrived this morning there was a big article next to me – telling me all about me – when I was born – what I did, when I died, but suddenly the article just slipped off the page – and here I am – jolly odd. Not knowing. |

| Alice | ? You're dead? |

| Scientist | Yes. ? Aren't you? |

| Alice | No. |

| Scientist | ! Oh! Everyone else on this page is. How strange. |

| Alice | Perhaps, you were a scientist or an inventor. |

Scientist   Yes. *[The Scientist looks at his\her white coat.]*

Let's hope I invented something useful – or even good.

It would be horrible to discover one had invented something

really silly, like – like the Hula Hoop.

Alice   I don't think they're silly. I used to like them –

when I was little of course.

Scientist   But they're not exactly important either, ? are they?

? How did you get here?

Alice   I fell … no … I tripped. I'm just … passing through.

Scientist   Well, everyone is dear, everyone is.

Alice   And I need to find my way out.

Scientist   ? The way out? I don't think there is a way out.

Best thing you can do is get those Vowels back into line –

if you have any influence that it is.

Alice   ? Me?

 **EX 1**   There she is.

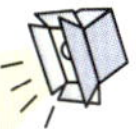

> *Once again Alice runs on the spot. The dead scientist*
> *fades from view as more Exclamation Marks enter.*
> *For a moment, it is rather like a Hollywood musical as*
> *all the Exclamation Marks form a line and chase Alice.*
> *The chasers can include the Ballerina, the Model,*
> *and the Footballers.*
> *As they catch her there is climatic music.*

 **EX1**   ? And you are?

Alice   Alice.

 **EX 1**   You Alice are in big trouble. ! Attention!

> *All the Exclamation Marks stand to attention.*

Model   That's her – she's the one.

EX 1   Quiet in court. All rise.

> *They all stand on tiptoe.*

Alice   I'd just like to say …

All ! Silence!!!!!!!!!!!!!

Drum beat. Enter three Question Marks.
One with a huge wig, the others with smaller wigs.

QM 1 ? Is this she?

EX 1 It is, your honour.

QM 1 ? Will you sit down?

Alice There isn't a chair.

QM 1 That is the correct answer. Continue in that manner and all will be well, despite the darkness of the day. Sit.

QM1 signals for a chair. Alice sits.

QM 1 Begin.

The other two QM's come up to her.

QM 2 ? Your name?

Alice Alice.

 **QM 2**   ? Spelt?

Alice   A.

 **QM 2**   ? A?

Alice   L.I.C.E.

QM 2   Lice.

So you are – A. Lice

Alice   No, not a lice. Alice.

QM 2   ? Where are you Alice?

Alice   I'm – well – I think … I'm in the news.

QM 1   ? You think? You've been running from one page to the next like a greyhound – or that horse – who won yesterday.
Of course you're in the news. I'm in the news – we're all in the news. ? Can you please answer some sensible questions?

QM 3   ? Are you a picture?

Alice   No.

 **QM 3** ? In that case you don't belong here do you?

Alice ? Is that important?

 **QM 2** ? Do you want to belong here ... Alice?

Alice No. Not really.

The crowd mutters darkly.

Alice I want to go home.

 **QM 1** In that case you shouldn't have left 'home'.

Alice I haven't left home – I'm only ten.

 **EX 1** Silence.

 **QM 2** ? How did you get here?

Alice Through a hole, actually.

 **QM 3** ? A hole?

 **QM 1** Newspapers don't have holes. Cheese has holes, clothes have holes, rabbits have holes.
Newspapers do not on the whole ... have holes.

Alice	Well, this one did.
EX 1	Silence.
QM 2	? Are you innocent?

Silence.

| QM 2 | ? Let me ask the question a different way, are you guilty? |

Silence.

QM 1	Don't be confused child – it's the same question.
Alice	? How can I answer? I have to be silent.
EX 1	Silence.
Alice	You see.
QM 1	Yes, quite. *[He turns to EX 1]*
	The silences in this court are far too loud.
	Now answer the question Alice.
Alice	I'm innocent.

  **QM 2 & 3**

? Why?

Alice

Because I'm not guilty.

 **QM 3**

? Not guilty of what?

Alice

Anything. I'm just – here.

The crowd mutter darkly.

 **QM 1**

In a place you should not be, that does not belong to you or you to it. Since your arrival, there has been nothing but chaos and confusion.

Alice

But it's nothing to do with me … it was the Vowels.

QM 1

! Ah! The Vowels.

Alice

And now really – I want to go home – please.

QM 1

Bring on the Vowels.

Alice

I don't like this newspaper – and I want to go home. I want to go home now.

 **EX 1**   *[Whispers]* Silence.

Alice   I will not be silent anymore.

 **QM 1**   Be quiet child – or you will force my hand.

Alice   I will not be silenced.

 **QM 1**   Silence the child.

> *Alice is then forcibly gagged, although she puts up a good fight. The Vowels are brought on. They are made to kneel. They have hoods over their heads.*

 **QM 2**   ? Have you ever met any of these – Vowels?

Alice   *[Mutters under her gag]*

 **QM 3**   Speak more clearly child.

Alice   *[Mutters through the gag]*

 **QM 1**   Alice – this is very serious – ? did you talk to these Vowels for any length of time?

Alice   *[Mutters]*

QM 1   ? And did you tell them that they were 'the resistance' –
the only hope, and they should fight for every column inch –
every article, every story – until the terrible words
were no more?

This sends shock waves around the court.

Surely Alice – you must see that the whole point of being
a letter is to be in words. ? Is it not? Take off their hoods.

*The hoods are taken off the Vowels who blink in the
light, and are scared.*

QM 1   If you see the girl, with a [red dress/ trousers] on,
who persuaded you to rebel – then point to her.

They all point at Alice.

The crowd shout at Alice, calling for her death.

QM 1   Ssh now. Before I pass a properly constructed sentence –
? have you any last thing to say?

Alice   [mutters] 'I'm innocent.'

 **QM 2**   Didn't catch that.

 **QM 3**   Nor me.

 **QM 1**   Alice – you will be taken from this court to the place

of execution – where you will be questioned – to death,

and may God have mercy on your soul.

Take her to the place of execution.

They move her chair forward six inches.

 **QM 1**   Proceed.

**Get the children to think up their own puzzling questions to do with anything going on in the world at the time of the production or use the ones below or a mixture of the two.*

 **QM 2**   ? What is your favourite colour?

 **QM 3**   ? Do you like jackets or chips?

 **QM 3**   ? Was this the paper you fell into?

 **QM 2**   ? Why did you run away?

 **QM 3**   ? Is this the hole?

QM 3   ? Why do you say 'actually' at the end of sentences?

QM 2   ? Have you had chicken pox?

QM 3   ? Why are the ice caps melting?

QM 2   ? Do you know what's important?

QM 3   ? Why are you so angry?

QM 2   ? Do you want to grow up?

QM 2   ? Do you have a best friend?

QM 3   ? Why are you so polite?

QM 2   ? Why are you so rude?

QM 2   ? What do you care about?

QM 3   ? Do you love your family?

QM 3   ? Will the war be over by Christmas?

QM 2   ? Do you think you're better than everyone else?

QM 3   ? Or less important?

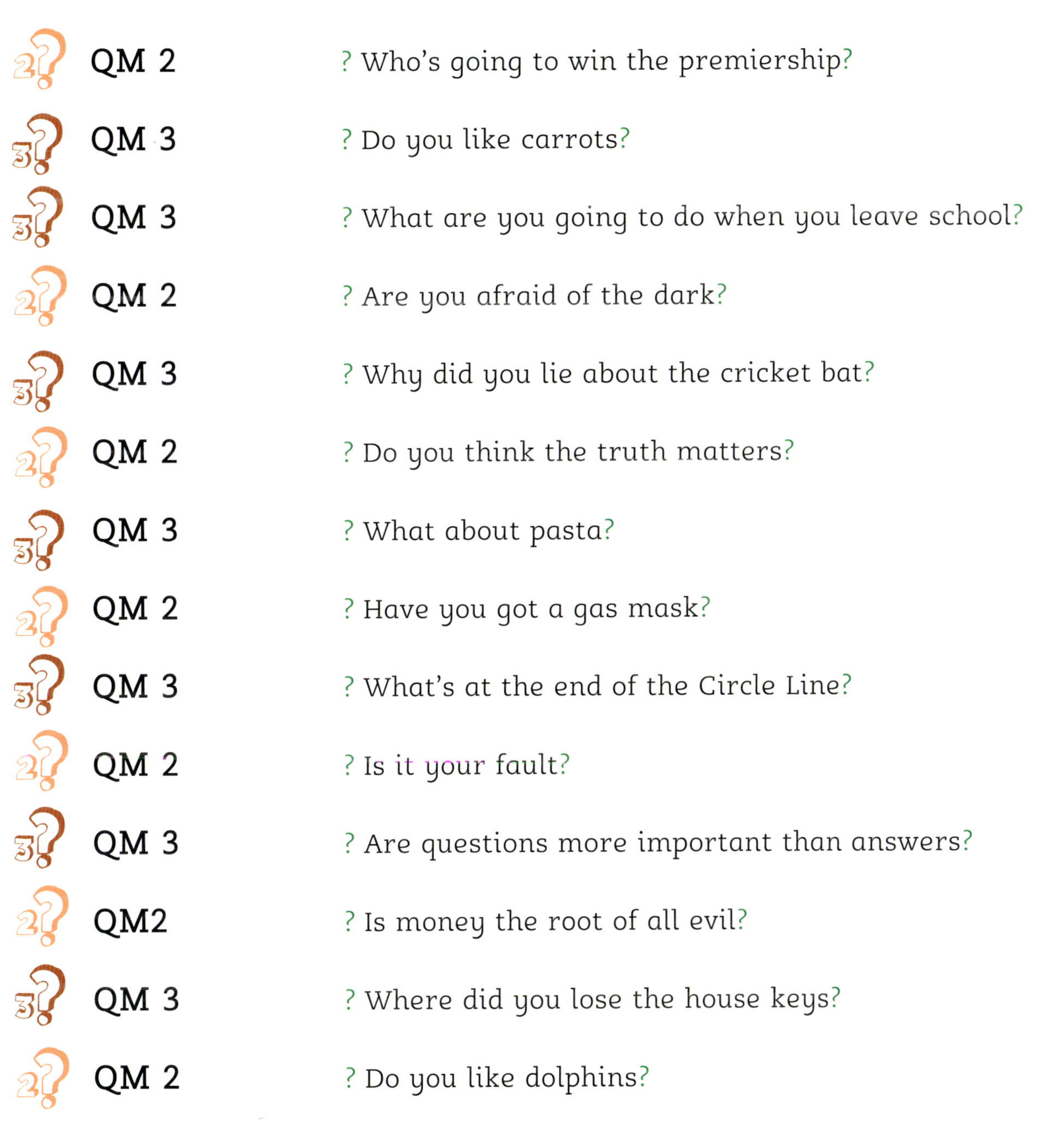

QM 2	? Who's going to win the premiership?
QM 3	? Do you like carrots?
QM 3	? What are you going to do when you leave school?
QM 2	? Are you afraid of the dark?
QM 3	? Why did you lie about the cricket bat?
QM 2	? Do you think the truth matters?
QM 3	? What about pasta?
QM 2	? Have you got a gas mask?
QM 3	? What's at the end of the Circle Line?
QM 2	? Is it your fault?
QM 3	? Are questions more important than answers?
QM2	? Is money the root of all evil?
QM 3	? Where did you lose the house keys?
QM 2	? Do you like dolphins?

? Where is Northampton? 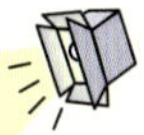

During this questioning, Alice is given the paper she
fell into and she has an idea, she starts to rip it up.
All the letters and pictures and punctuation stumble
from side to side like sailors in a storm, but every time
they get near Alice, she rips up the paper some more.
They cry out and end up in a messy pile on the floor.
Alice rips off the gag over her mouth and starts to run,
still getting nowhere fast.

Lights fade to black out.

—The END—

Teachers Notes

First read through

Once you have cast the play and are ready to read it through, get the actors to work through it in real detail. Establish the fact that every play is a story and it is everybody's job to tell it.

Introduce the rule that in order to keep the reading alive, everyone needs to bring the same focus, listening skills and conviction to it as the actor who is actually speaking. Energy, focus and clarity are really important. If the actors understand what they are saying, why they are speaking and to whom they are speaking, they are going to be more audible.

Don't get them to learn their lines and come off the script until they have asked all the questions they need to ask.

Emphasise the need to speak the lines as they are written. The writer has chosen her words very carefully and the play will be less good if the lines are approximated or edited in any way.

At the very first reading, encourage them to make eye contact with the character they are speaking to. If their lines are directed at the whole company they must make it obvious. Establish which moments are private and which are public and to the audience.

Here are a few **concentration exercises** you might try out with the group as a warm up exercise.

In a circle - standing

Ask the group to pass a clap around the circle in sequence. The aim is for it to go round at high speed; each member needs to receive the clap before passing it on. Take a stopwatch and time the speed it takes to pass the clap around, try improving on the group's record. Vary the clap direction. To make it more complicated and encourage eye contact, introduce passing the clap across the circle.

In a circle - seated

The aim is for each member of the group to stand up one at a time saying their name. If two or more stand or speak at the same time, then the exercise has to start again. Everyone needs to make eye contact and listen intently because even the smallest hesitation is not allowed. Nor is it permitted for the group to stand one at a time in sequence around the circle. Once everyone is on his or her feet, the exercise can be repeated in reverse with each member sitting down.

Knowing the plot

Split the class into groups of five. Give the groups five to ten minutes to work together and create a short movie trailer for the play. Ask the groups to find five images that represent the play: one before the play starts, three during the course of the play and one after the play ends. Get them to present the tableaux to the other groups but in the wrong order. Ask the other groups to caption the images and put them in the right order.

Decide which were the most striking and accurate images. Was there an image that successfully captured the essence of the whole play?

Understanding what the play is about

In a circle

Moving around the circle ask each actor to say a word that they associate with the play. Encourage the group to be spontaneous, if someone cannot think of a word, they should simply say the title of the play. A more confident group might enjoy raising the stakes with this exercise by throwing a ball or beanbag around the circle, whoever catches it has to throw in their idea.

If some of the ideas seem unrelated to the play, discuss them afterwards and encourage the actor to explain the link.

In groups

Ask each group to draw nine images from the play. Ask them to decide who the central character is in each image. Get them to say what the character wants from the scene. Give each scene a title.
The outcomes might be as follows with possible variations.

1 Alice wants to find out what's wrong with her dad and the people on the bus

2 The Consonants want to stop the Vowels from leaving the words

3 The Consonants want everything to calm down

4 Alice wants to go home

5 The Model wants to know who she is

6 Child One and Child Two want to be safe

7 The scientist on the obituary page wants to know he had a useful life

8 The newspaper characters want Alice to die

9 Alice wants to escape from the news

This exercise can be developed. In each picture the groups might look at all the characters and where each of their wants conflict with the wants of the others. Decide what the super objective might be if all of the objectives in the play were put together- e.g. everyone wants to be safe.

Themes

The play contains the following themes. You might like to discuss them.

- Fear and worry about the modern world

- Use of language

- Change in language (are vowels disappearing because of text messaging?)

- The power of the media

- Being in the wrong place at the wrong time

Cross-curricular work

Take a current broadsheet newspaper. Have groups look at the international, arts, fashion, sports and obituary pages. Ask them to compare who is featured currently with the characters featured in the play. Get the group to identify the vowels, consonants, exclamation marks etc. in the print.

Although the plays stands alone and doesn't necessarily require the group to have pre knowledge of *Alice In Wonderland* it would be interesting for them to have access to this children's classic or one of the film or animated versions of it.

Here is a **speaking and listening exercise** you might try out. It is useful for focusing the whole group.

Take the words 'diddly' and 'dee'. Get the group to stand in a circle. Each person says one of the words and passes it round the circle in the direction in which the speaker is looking. Build up to constant changes of direction. Aim for an unbroken rhythm with no hesitations which might go something like this – diddly dee diddly dee diddly dee diddly diddly dee dee dee diddly dee diddly dee etc. Anyone hesitating is out!

Exercises and improvisations around the play

There is great scope for invention in this play. Here are some exercises that enhance the group's capacity to **work together physically** and use the acting space more efficiently.

Get the group to walk around the space using all of it. If anyone sees an empty space they should occupy it. Get the group to walk at normal pace and then very gradually speed up to a gentle run while still making sure all of the spaces are filled. It's much harder to fill the space at speed and they must on no account bump into one another. Get them to gradually reduce their speed until they are stationary.

Ask the group to move slowly into a circle, don't allow any discussion. They must make the shape by co-operating with everyone else. Once you're satisfied with this shape ask them to form others. Finally, get them to form a perfect square. Have them imagine the square is balanced on a pin.

Get the half the group (B) to choose a partner (A) without letting the partner know who they are (it doesn't matter if more than one person chooses the same partner). A is a bomb, so the partner must keep as far away as possible while trying, along with the rest of the group, to keep the square balanced on the pin.

Repeat the exercise choosing two partners. Again, don't let them know who they are. Try and make a triangle as the three all move around the space.

Now do the bomb and shield game. (A) chooses one partner who wants to get him/her and a second partner who will be A's shield. (A) must move around the space trying to keep the shield between her/him and the bomb.

Brainstorm what physical attributes the consonants, vowels, exclamation and question marks might have. Work out how they would move in a group and as individuals. Decide what shape they might assume when stationary. They might move in straight lines or create floor patterns.

Encourage the group to work on different levels, the vowels might move closer to the floor for instance. The different groups might move at different speeds.

In groups, take a close look at some of the moments in the play that need to be achieved physically.

- When a short cold wind blows across the street and everyone except Alice is blown away

- When there's a sudden cry and sucking noise and Alice falls in a spin into the newspaper

- When Alice starts to rip up the paper, all the letters and pictures and punctuation stumble from side to side, but every time they get near Alice she rips up the paper some more. They cry and end up in a messy pile on the floor.

Encourage the actors to be inventive with the sound effects.

Humour is very important in this play but it's important to give it a nightmarish quality. Once the groups have worked out these sequences get them to make them as surreal as possible. Look at the very ending when Alice runs without getting anywhere. Have the group experiment with slow motion, at times Alice might be moving at a much slower speed than the other characters.

Character work

There are twenty-five characters in the play. You could add more punctuation characters and consonants. It's vital that the girl playing Alice is very watchable.

The whole group might begin by collectively brainstorming approaches to the characters.

Deciding what part of the body each character might lead from

- Nose – might be a snob or inquisitive

- Chest – butch/proud/confident

- Belly button – lazy/stupid/slow/sluggish

A character might be pulled backwards by the bottom while leading with the nose.

Try out these seven levels of **tension** with the group. Get them to make up their own title for each.

1 Can hardly move (jellyfish?)

2 Really laid back

3 Slow bumbling/short attention span/quite good humoured

4 Really together

5 Alert

6 Tense (type of energy you'd have if there was a suspected bomb in the room)

7 Complete debilitating tension

This exercise is a good starting point when creating a character and charting a character's journey through the play. Get the group to decide what level of tension Alice might have at any given point.

Ask each member of the group to choose a character from the play. Ask them to create a physical representation of the character when they first enter. For instance, if it were a colour what colour would it be? If it were an animal what would it be? Have them move around the space as that animal. Now ask them to be 50% animal and 50% human. Ask them to go back to their character and keep some of the animal characteristics they were pleased with.

Design

Keep this as simple as you can. Your main objective is to define the difference between the real world and the nightmarish world.

This could be achieved by painting a super real backcloth in bright and bold colours with images of domesticity on it. Alice's dad's chair is enough to indicate this. Alice's fall through the hole in the newspaper might be achieved by introducing gauze with faint newspaper print on it in front of the backcloth. The audience would be dimly aware of the real world behind the gauze.

The rest of the cast might have costumes based on newspaper print; Alice should stand out by remaining in her ordinary clothes in distinctive colours as she enters the newspaper world. When creating the acting areas avoid leaving centre stage, the most powerful and useful location, uninhabited.

Make your costume design as big and bold as you can. Give each actor a body size piece of paper (we recommend decorator's lining paper roll torn in strips). Get the actor to lie down and have someone draw around the body shape. Take a wax crayon and draw the initial costume design onto the paper. Get the group to choose the football strip for the team in the play.

Drama and the Dyslexic Learner

For some dyslexics, drama lessons and other opportunities to perform, provide the ultimate in multi-sensory experience. It is perhaps for this reason that, despite their difficulties, many dyslexics find themselves drawn to the worlds of theatre and cinema. How and why is this possible?

Dyslexia has been described as a gift … and it is certainly true that many dyslexics are very creative in the fields of art, music and drama. They tend to see the 'big picture', they don't always want to do things the conventional way, and the results can be stunning.

Being involved in a drama production gives the opportunity to step into another role, to become another person and this can provide a safe environment to push out barriers, to explore and experiment without fear of making mistakes as 'yourself'. There is no right or wrong and by working as part of a group, each participant has a part in the decision making. It is an ideal activity in which to work on social skills, interaction, understanding of non-verbal communication, sharing and taking leadership roles.

Hints for working with dyslexics

Establish a clear and regular rehearsal time
Reward and praise those who turn up on time particularly in the early stages.

Use the warm up exercises to enhance confidence and to break down barriers by indirectly working on inhibitions.

Free them from the text as soon as possible
Describe a scenario and encourage them to explore it using their own words and movements.
Explore aspects of character by working in twos and role-playing.
Dyslexics 'see' ideas and situations in pictures … get them to visualise themselves in particular situations.
The more work they do in pairs and small groups, the more confidence they will gain to perform for others.

Return to the text and work with them to become familiar with it
Read through small sections at a time. It doesn't work to have a whole play read-through. This is too tiring and stressful.

Locating their words will be much easier using the new Barrington Stoke design in which parts are identified through the use of icons and colours. **Stage Directions** stand out in the spotlights on the right hand side of the page.

Learning words will probably take longer for dyslexics. Some will not be familiar with play text and will need reminding that they **will also need to memorise** the final words of the actor who comes immediately before them.

Make sure that you check their comprehension of the script and clarify any new concepts and words. Do not underestimate the power of learning their words by chanting them over and over again as they walk up and down. This makes it a visual, auditory and kinaesthetic experience.

Practice sections of text in small groups to familiarise them with the words.

As soon as this familiarisation has begun, **begin to work on moves**. Many dyslexics learn by association so they will find it easier to link **what they say with how and where they move**.

This will be further reinforced by use of **props and sound effects**. These should be introduced fairly early on … not left until words and moves are secure. The dyslexic needs the whole picture to aid his/her learning.

Some dyslexics will need their words **on tape or CD**, but remember to put the **other parts on too**.

If music is to be used in the performance, leave plenty of time to rehearse this. Individual songs should be learned first, and incorporated into rehearsals when the singers are confident. Dyslexics are usually quite good at learning songs because they associate words with the music, **but** there may be a problem if there are several verses that **sound** the same, but have different words. The sequence of verses will need particular strategies … best devised by the singer.

Beware of wanting a whole cast to sway from left to right to music. **Dyslexics find this unbelievably difficult**. It can be done, but it will need a lot of work and a lot of practice.

Stage sets and large props will be the pegs that the dyslexic hangs his/her performance on. **Don't make changes**, particularly in the last few rehearsals. **Remember** change will throw the dyslexic actor.

If possible, **allow for 2 or 3 rehearsals with costumes** to help them get used to performing in them. In many cases, the sooner the actors can be dressed, the better.

Don't wait for the technical rehearsal to introduce **lights and sound effects**. They need longer to get used to these.

Don't forget those who are working back-stage. This is a crucial role and can make or break a performance. It can be a good way in to performance for the dyslexic with very low self-confidence.

Stage design, lighting and the making of props are all areas which may appeal to the stage shy dyslexic. Harnessing their artistic talents can result in innovative and impressive interpretations and raise their self-esteem sufficiently to tempt them into taking a role in a future production.

Props people and **costume** helpers will **need lists**. It can be helpful to have different colour labels for each character's costumes and props.

Older students working as stage managers and in the lighting bay will need **clear instructions**, and adult supervision.

Stage-hands and front of house people need rehearsals too. Do not expect them to do these jobs for the first time when there is an audience. Performances cannot happen without these important tasks being done well. It can be the perfect way to raise someone's self-esteem.

At the end of a show it is a good idea to produce certificates for **ALL** those who have taken part, to recognise the effort they have made as well as the success of the show itself.

And finally ...

Some dyslexics really come alive when they have that audience in front of them. They love performing and enjoy the power they have to make their audience laugh or cry. Freed from the restrictions of the written word they can address issues from which they have previously shied away with brilliant results, and that's why they love to do it!

Edwina Cole
November 2003

Stanbridge Earls School, Romsey, Hampshire

Barrington Stoke would like to thank the following people:

Anthony Banks for his insight and original idea of publishing plays for the reluctant reader.
Edwina Cole for her expertise in using drama to promote self-esteem with dyslexics.
Tom Kirkham for sharing his teaching ideas. Jim Mulligan for interviewing the playwrights.
The writers, teachers and Drama co-ordinators who brought the plays to life at the Retreat
in Keswick, November 2003. And above all Suzy Graham-Adriani, Will Critzman and the team
at the National who have brought both expertise and fun to the whole project.

Published in 2004 in Great Britain by

Barrington Stoke Ltd, Sandeman House, Trunk's Close,

55 High Street, Edinburgh EH1 1SR

www.barringtonstoke.co.uk

Copyright © 2004 Charles Way

ISBN 1-84299-170-1

Edited by Julia Rowlandson

Designed and typeset by Helen Ferguson at Lucy Richards Design

Printed in China

If you enjoyed this, why not try these...

More 20 minute plays for Primary Schools from Barrington Stoke

The Willow Pattern by Judith Johnson
The traditional story in which Knoon-she pursues her love for Chang against her father's wishes.

Jeremy and The Thinking Machine
by Janet Neipris and Barbara Greenberg
A play with music. The life of Jeremy Jayjay, reluctant heir to the Kingdom of Jamboreen, changes when he meets his crazy fairy godmother with her magical thinking machine.

The Gift of the Gab by Christina Reid
Communicating with the Yackety Yaks is a tough business until the Great Gab intervenes with the trusty team of Lingoes.

Daffodil Scissors by Philip Ridley
(Also suitable for Lower secondary pupils)
Bullying, a needy mum and a lack of social skills make life hard for Daffodil until he meets the Bag Lady.

Alice in the News by Charles Way
(Also suitable for Lower secondary pupils)
Alice, trapped in a newspaper, becomes involved in a dispute between the vowels and the consonants.

Title	Author	ISBN	Price	Qty	Total £
The Willow Pattern	Judith Johnson	1-842991-67-1	£4.99		
Pack of 8 copies		1-842992-23-6	£39.92		
Jeremy and The Thinking Machine	Janet Neipris and Barbara Greenberg	1-842991-71-X	£4.99		
Pack of 8 copies		1-842992-24-4	£39.92		
The Gift of the Gab	Christina Reid	1-842991-68-X	£4.99		
Pack of 8 copies		1-842992-25-2	£39.92		
Daffodil Scissors	Philip Ridley	1-842991-69-8	£4.99		
Pack of 8 copies		1-842992-26-0	£39.92		
Alice in the News	Charles Way	1-842991-70-1	£4.99		
Pack of 8 copies		1-842992-27-9	£39.92		
Total Payment					

Your Details

Name _______________________________

Job Title _______________________________

School Name _______________________________

Address _______________________________

____

____

Postcode _______________________________

Telephone _______________________________

Email _______________________________

Method of Payment

☐ Please invoice my school

☐ I enclose a cheque (payable to Macmillan Distribution Ltd)

☐ Credit Card Type** _______________________________

Number _______________________________

Expiry Date _______________________________

** We are sorry but Macmillan do not accept Switch

Please send your order to Macmillan Distribution Ltd, Brunel Road, Houndmills, Basingstoke, Hampshire, RG21 6XS
Tel 01256 302 699 **Fax** 01256 812 558
email mdl@macmillan.co.uk **online** www.barringtonstoke.co.uk
For further information ring Barrington Stoke on **0131 557 2020**